FIGHTER PILOT

With grateful thanks to Ron Jess for sharing his first-hand experiences. Thanks also to Stuart Hadaway of the Royal Airforce Museum, London.

Reprinted 2007
First published 2007 by
A & C Black Publishers Ltd
38 Soho Square, London, W1D 3HB

www.acblack.com

ISBN 978-0-7136-7773-7 (hbk)
ISBN 978-0-7136-7772-0 (pbk)

A CIP catalogue for this book is available
from the British Library.

This book is produced using paper that is made from
wood grown in managed, sustainable forests. It is natural,
renewable and recyclable. The logging and manufacturing
processes conform to the environmental regulations
of the country of origin.

Printed and bound by MPG Books Ltd, Bodmin, Cornwall.

TOUGH JOBS
FIGHTER PILOT

Helen Greathead
Illustrated by Bob Dewar

A & C Black · London

Welcome to World War 2

Imagine a time, not so long ago, when:

- All the big countries in the world were at war.
- At night, whole cities turned out the lights to hide from enemy bombers.
- City children were sent to the country, away from harm — and away from their parents.

- The law said you could only have nine sweets a week!
- Your old pots, pans and garden railings were taken away to make planes and guns.
- Eighteen-year-old boys were being called up to join the army, the navy and the air force.

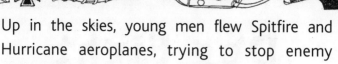

Up in the skies, young men flew Spitfire and Hurricane aeroplanes, trying to stop enemy aircraft from reaching their targets.

Down below, people watched and cheered on the flying heroes. Soon every boy had the same dream – to be a fighter pilot.

World War 2 ended over 60 years ago. It lasted only six years, but it was a terrible time in history. It was the biggest war *ever*. Millions of people died all over the world. And for millions more, life would never be the same again.

Dog Fight

Let's pretend you live in the 1940s. Britain is at war with Germany, and air battles are happening in the sky right over your head!

Today you are playing in the garden, when you hear an angry buzzing noise in the distance. You spot three planes swooping across the sky in a real, live dogfight.

Two of the planes are German Messerschmitts. Only one plane is British. But you can see it's a Spitfire. Hurray! Spitfires are the best planes *ever*.

With a *du-du-du*, the Messerschmitts shoot at the Spitfire. Suddenly, bullets hit the Spitfire and a stream of smoke pours from its engine. The plane is heading for the woods – nose first!

The Germans are flying away. They think they've shot down the Spitfire. But suddenly, the plane pulls straight and flies towards the fields behind the woods, where it can land. Phew, the pilot is safe!

Your heart is still racing as you rush inside. "Mum, did you see that?" you shout.

Your mum doesn't waste time watching the dogfights. She mostly sleeps and does housework during the day, then she's out being an air-raid precautions (ARP) warden most nights.

She makes sure no one's lights are showing. If enemy planes spot them, they might attack! She has to get people to the shelters when the air-raid siren sounds, too. Your dad is away in the navy.

You love living where you do. You can watch the action in the skies from your own home. Your mum tells you all the latest news when she comes off duty. And, best of all, the government has turned the farm at the end of your lane into an airbase!

You don't have to go to school any more. You have lessons with an old schoolteacher instead. But you're only interested in one subject … how to be a fighter pilot.

You're not old enough to fly a plane yet, and you can't be sure you'd be picked for the job. But you do have a plan. You're going to find out as much as you can about fighter planes and fighter pilots.

Then, when the time comes, the RAF won't dare turn you down.

A few days later, you're outside when a truck full of new recruits rattles down the lane. They're heading for the airbase. It's too good a chance to miss...

You grab your gas mask and run after the truck, waving and grinning at the boys. One of them spots you. He shouts to the driver to stop, then stretches out his arm to help you up!

"I've a brother at home just like you," says an American.

"Must be a cheeky wee monkey," adds a friendly Scotsman.

The boys all talk with different accents. There's a Frenchman, and a cross-looking man from Poland, too. They're in with boys from all over Britain.

The truck stops at the airbase gates. The guard doesn't spot you hiding behind the boys' legs. You can hardly believe your luck. At last, you're just where you want to be … inside the RAF airbase!

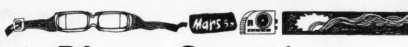

Plane Spotting...

...was a popular hobby during World War 2. It was also part of a pilot's job. You needed to know which plane was which, or you might shoot down one of your own!

Spitfire: single-seat fighter plane
Strong points: great at high-altitude flying
Problem: a bit wobbly when firing

Hurricane: single-seat fighter plane
Strong points: can still fly when badly damaged
Problem: doesn't fly well at high altitudes

Bristol Beaufighter: two-seat night fighter
Strong points: radar tracks approaching planes
Problem: unsteady on takeoff and landing

Messerschmitt BF109: single-seat fighter plane
Strong points: flies fast, climbs and dives very well
Problem: only carries enough fuel for ten minutes' fighting over England

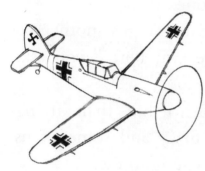

Junkers 88: Dive bomber and night fighter
Strong points: fast for its size
Problem: slower than one-man fighter planes and needs a three-man crew

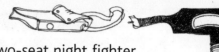

New Boys

"So how did you all get to be pilots?" you ask eagerly, as the boys jump down from the truck.

"I didn't," says one.

"We're not all daft," laughs another.

"Then why are you here?" you ask, confused.

"There's more to life than flying planes," says the first, "and some of us reckon we're too young to die."

"Besides," says the Scot, "every pilot needs ground crew for support." He introduces you to the boys.

"Meet Tommy and Vince, both trained mechanics. We need them to fix the planes and keep them flying. Bert and

Johnnie are wireless operators – they keep contact with the pilots during takeoff and landing. Jim is our cook. I'm Scottie," he touches his shoulder and you notice his wings. "I *am* one of the daft ones – a pilot. So are Tomasz, Reg, Buck and François. We call him French Frank."

You're dying to ask more questions, but suddenly you're interrupted.

"What are you doing here and how did you get onto the airbase?" A flying officer is questioning you.

Scottie quickly answers on your behalf. "He's my cousin. Lives down the road. I said I'd show him around."

The officer looks cross, but he can see you're not a German spy. He orders everyone back onto the truck for a tour of the airfield. You climb on, too, and he doesn't say anything.

The truck drives down the side of the long landing strip, but you hardly see any planes. In the centre of the field stands the control tower, where the wireless operators and flying control personnel work.

You're surprised to see the pigsties are still standing, and wonder why you're stopping outside them.

"These are the nissen huts where you'll sleep," the officer tells the boys.

You are horrified. Flying heroes shouldn't have to sleep in a pigsty – even if it does have a fancy name!

Inside, the boys share bedrooms, a common room and a cold-water tap.

Across the field, there are washrooms, toilets and a mess hall, where the boys can find food, drink and entertainment. There's even a cinema!

"Now let's see some planes," says the officer.

You rattle off in the truck again. Then, just as it stops, you hear a sudden, deafening wailing sound. The air-raid siren – and you couldn't be anywhere more dangerous!

In seconds, the boys are off the truck. You jump down, trip over and land face first on the muddy airfield.

French Frank and Reg grab you and throw you into what looks like a small hill. Your gas mask whacks you on the head, slips out of its bag and slides across the ground.

"This is one of our new E-pens," says the officer, as you struggle to push the mask back into the bag. "We used to keep the planes in neat rows on the field.

It was a bit like asking German bombers to help themselves! Now the planes are hidden by these bunkers, they're harder to spot and there's plenty of cover for the crew."

"Head down," yells the officer.

A huge German Junkers 88 whizzes past so close you could almost touch the tip of its wing. It dots the field with machine-gun fire. Then the pilot spots a Spitfire, the doors open in the belly of his plane, and he litters the field with bombs...

They miss the plane, but leave big craters in the airfield!

You've never seen a German plane up close, and you've never been so near to a bomb! It's exciting, but scary, and you can't wait to tell your mum. But then you remember – she doesn't know where you are! When you get home you'll be in big, big trouble.

Call Up

Most boys are called up to fight at 18. If you volunteer first, you can choose between the army, the navy and the Royal Air Force (RAF).

The RAF is picky. It likes you best if you:

• have been in the Air Training Corps – which prepares boys for the RAF from the age of 16
• are 100% fit – you need perfect eyesight for flying and perfect hearing
• have been to a good school
• are very clever.

If you are all these things, you could be offered a ground job, or become:

Bomb aimer   Radio operator
      Air gunner   Navigator

Oh and there's just a small chance they might choose you to be a pilot. You have be able to react fast and have excellent hand, eye and foot co-ordination.

As a bomber pilot you'll fly with a crew, who navigate, drop the bombs and fire the guns.

As a fighter pilot you'll have to fly, navigate and fight all by yourself – it's a very TOUGH JOB.

Scramble!

"You're lucky only one plane attacked the base," your mum says when she finds out what happened. "Some airfields have been completely destroyed by German bombers. If I find out you've been there again, you're going straight to Wales."

Most of your class has been evacuated to Wales, but your mum didn't want you to go. And you certainly don't want to be away from your mum – or the dogfights.

She has a point about the airbase. Trouble is, if you're ever going to be a fighter pilot, you've got to get back there and find out more.

Getting in a second time isn't so easy. You keep returning to the airbase but the guards won't let you through the gates. It's two weeks before you're lucky again – the pilot officer sees you and winks.

"Here to see your cousin?" he says. "Come on, then, we'd better let you in."

The pilots look tired. They're lounging around outside the mess, listening to music and waiting.

A Spitfire buzzes about above your head. It flies in circles, seems to drop out of the sky, then zooms back up. Then it spirals down, almost to the ground, before shooting up and flipping over again and again.

"He's one of our ace pilots," says Scottie, nodding towards the plane as he sees you.

"An ace is a pilot who's shot down five or more enemy planes," explains Reg.

"I bet you wish you could fly like that," you say to Scottie.

"You cheeky wee monkey," Scottie laughs. "We can all fly like that!"

Jim arrives with a trolley loaded with tea, bread, jam and the most butter you've seen since war began.

"We have to look after our fighter boys," says Jim.

But Scottie pushes the biggest slice your way. It's delicious!

The Spitfire has come in to land, and the ace hops out and heads straight for the tea trolley. You're desperate to talk to him.

"Um, h-h-how can I become a b-brilliant pilot like you?" you stammer.

"Carrots," says the pilot. "Eat plenty of 'em."

Everyone laughs as he strides off, but you don't get the joke.

"Carrots are supposed to be good for your eyesight," French Frank explains. "So you can spot enemy planes before they spot you."

"So what else did you do in training?" you ask, changing the subject.

"Lots of square bashing," says Reg.

"That's marching up and down," Scottie whispers.

"We had to study hard before they let us near an aeroplane," says Buck.

"Like what?" you ask.

"Well, there was theory of flying, air navigation, how the instrument panel works," Buck says. "Aircraft recognition was the best!"

"I had English lessons," adds French Frank, "so that ground control could understand me over the radio."

"What about your first flight?" you ask. "It must have been exciting stepping into a Spitfire for the first time."

"Nobody starts training in a Spitfire," Scottie grins. "They only carry one person. You need a plane with a second seat and a second set of controls for your instructor – if you want to live!"

"My first flight was in one of these," says Reg, pointing to a picture in his book. "A Tiger Moth. I trained in Canada – it was my first time abroad."

"I got to train in an old bomber," chuckles Buck. "That plane was so big and heavy, I was surprised she ever got off the ground."

You hear a phone in the background and the boys are suddenly quiet. Then a bell rings, somebody yells "scramble!", and they all jump up. Tomasz strides out through the mess window. He looks really fierce. You notice Reg stuffing a teddy into his jacket pocket, whilst Buck is leaning over a bush – being sick!

"Gets to them in different ways," says Jim, as each pilot leaps into the cockpit of his plane. They take to the sky three at a time. "They've every reason to be scared," he continues, as the formation of planes rises up into the sky and then speeds away. "Who knows if we'll ever see them again."

Pilot Training

New pilots are sent to train abroad, where there's better weather and less chance of attack. But accidents happen wherever you are, and nearly as many boys die training as they do fighting.

Some pilots get to practise instrument flying on the ground in a Link Trainer with an instructor.

After 12 hours of flying instruction in a real aeroplane, you get to fly for ten minutes on your own! You'll build up to flying for three to four hours a day, and learn takeoff, landing, gliding, taxiing, flying upside down and aerobatics...

- loop (round in a circle)
- roll (turning the plane right over sideways)
- falling leaf (engine ticking over; plane flips first one side and then the other)

Aerobatics makes sure a pilot is in control of his machine, and can get out of almost any situation!

Flying training takes about two years. Fighter-pilot training should take up the last six months. But half-way through the war, there are too many pilots training, and not enough pilots fighting. So fighter training is cut to just weeks.

On the Inside

An hour later, you are walking home, thinking about what Jim said. You hope the boys are all right. As you reach the gate, you spot a Spitfire. It's flying so low you can see the pilot. It's Scottie. He's smiling and giving a thumbs–up sign. The mission was successful!

"Wish I could get up there," you say to Scottie the next day.

He winks and says, "Come with me." You walk over to an aircraft hangar. Mechanics are pushing out a Spitfire!

"Been working on her all night," says Vince, rubbing his eyes. "She's ready to go now. Look, we've added wing mirrors, so you can see bandits coming from behind."

"Can I fly in her?" you ask, jokingly.

"Nope," says Vince, "but you can sit inside."

One of the mechanics is filling up the Spitfire with fuel.

Underneath the fuel cap, you notice the plane has a name. "Why's she called Dorothy?" you laugh.

"All part of the war effort," Scottie answers. "Everyone wants to help buy more Spitfires. Each plane costs £5,000. A lot of girls called Dorothy gave money to buy this one."

"Right, kit on," says Scottie. "There's no heater in the cockpit, so this jacket will keep you warm!" He ties a silk scarf round your neck. "This will stop your neck rubbing against it. You'll be turning your head all the time, looking out for the enemy."

"You mean looking for bandits," you chip in.

"You're learning fast," says Scottie, slipping a life jacket over your head.

Scottie slides a step under Dorothy's wing. "Right foot on the step, left foot on the wing," he says.

But you get your legs mixed up. Scottie gives you a shove. "Foot on the fuselage," he continues, "then swing over into the cockpit."

You're facing the wrong way, but at least you're inside! Your heart is thundering as you turn around. There are knobs, buttons, dials and pedals everywhere. You have no idea what any of them do. And why is there a piece of potato wedged in the corner?

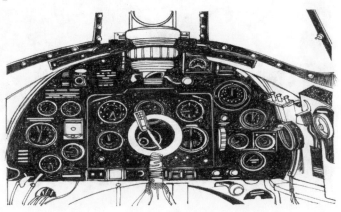

"Trick of the trade," says Scottie, climbing onto the wing. "Rub potato over the windscreen and it won't ice over when you fly really high."

Scottie straps you tightly into the harness, then slips something into your pocket. "First-aid kit," Scottie explains, "just in case you crash land!"

You gulp hard and try to pretend you're not worried.

"What happens if you want to … go," you whisper. Scottie pulls a tube from under your seat that leads outside the plane. You can't be expected to handle all the equipment and pee into that!

With your helmet on, Scottie shows you how to fit the mask over your face. He points to one of the dials. "When the altimeter hits 10,000 feet, you start breathing in oxygen through the mask," he explains. "If you don't you'll black out, and lose control of the plane."

Suddenly, there's a crackling noise in your ear, and you hear a familiar voice. "Hello, young Dorothy, ground control here." It's Bert – even he knows you're in the plane! "Are you ready to scramble?" It all feels very real, but you wish he wouldn't call you Dorothy.

Scottie nods. "Once you're cleared for takeoff, you pull the hand pump and press the starter buttons to get the engine going." He points them all out. "Now, feet on the rudder pedals." You slip off the seat to reach them. "And push the joystick forward." Your thumb settles on a cover over the red button, "Don't touch!" shouts Scottie, grabbing your arm. "That one fires the machine guns."

Suddenly, the cockpit slams shut, and you're alone in the Spitfire for a few thrilling minutes. There isn't much space, but there's an awful lot to look at.

Through the windscreen, you can't see much beyond the nose of the plane, but looking right, you spot a man walking quickly towards you. The cockpit flies open. "Out, quick!" yells Scottie. "Squadron Leader's coming!"

The Spitfire

People call the Spitfire the "sports car of the skies". It is a great fighter plane because it has a big engine, but its bodywork is small and light.

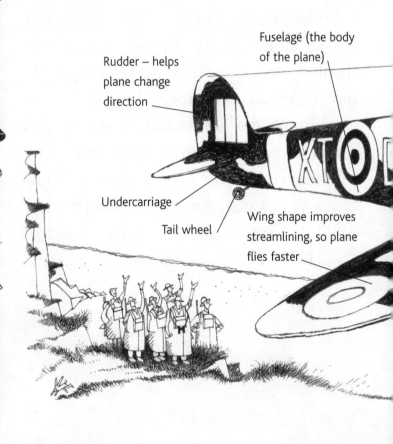

Fuselage (the body of the plane)

Rudder – helps plane change direction

Undercarriage

Tail wheel

Wing shape improves streamlining, so plane flies faster

It is easy for pilots to handle, especially during aerobatics. All through the war, Spitfire design changed and got better – by the end there were over 40 different models. Early Spitfires could fly up to 355 m.p.h. Later models could reach a fantastic 448 m.p.h.

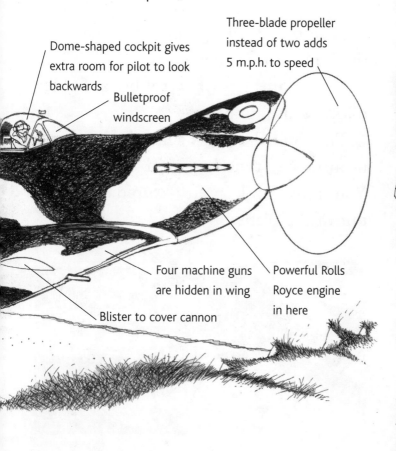

Three-blade propeller instead of two adds 5 m.p.h. to speed

Dome-shaped cockpit gives extra room for pilot to look backwards

Bulletproof windscreen

Four machine guns are hidden in wing

Blister to cover cannon

Powerful Rolls Royce engine in here

Up and Away

"What the devil's going on?" demands the Squadron Leader.

"I … um … want to be a fighter pilot," you mumble.

The Squadron Leader's thick, twirly moustache twitches and he laughs. You must look pretty stupid dangling out of the plane.

He helps you down. "Walk this way," he roars. "The name's Bentley-Smythe," he adds, sternly.

You follow him, shaking, around the back of the hangar to an aeroplane nearly twice as big as the Spitfire.

"She's a Bristol Beaufighter," Smythe explains. "A night fighter. She moves fast over long distances, attacks, and turns for home before the blighters know what's hit them. I'm test flying her. Fancy a ride?"

Wow! The day is getting better and better.

"I'll come, too," says Scottie, running up behind you. "To look after the boy," he adds. But you know he really wants to get inside the new plane.

Smythe tosses you each a parachute.

"If you need to release the parachute, get the ripcord in your right hand, but count slowly to ten first," says Scottie. "Try to pull your knees up to your chest just before landing."

Smythe climbs in through the roof of the cockpit. You and Scottie enter through a trapdoor underneath. You sit away from the cockpit, under a bubble window – the observer's lookout. Scottie crouches further down the tail. A funny-looking box with goggles on it hangs from the roof.

"The radar can pick up signals that tell us where enemy planes are and how fast they're moving," Scottie explains.

The engines roar, and the whole plane starts to shake as it rumbles along the ground. Suddenly, the nose lifts, the shaking stops and … you're flying!

You have to stretch to see out of the window. Down below, the airbase is getting smaller and smaller and … there's your house!

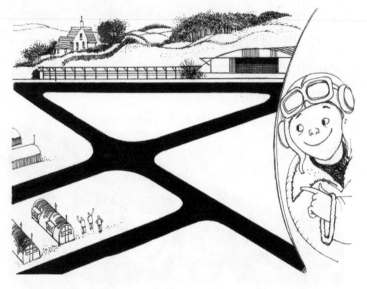

As you rise higher, you clip on your mask and dry oxygen tickles your throat. For the next half an hour, you watch and wonder. Above the clouds it's a different world.

"Flying is brilliant!" you cry over the noise of the engine.

"It's even better in a Spitfire," Scottie shouts back. "They're so light and easy to handle."

"Why do you need different types of fighter plane?" you ask.

"Different planes do different jobs." Scottie explains. "The Beaufighter carries powerful weapons and is good for long-range attacks. But a Spitfire is great for dogfights. A group of Spits can attack a huge formation of bombers, break them up and send them off target."

"What does it feel like to fight?" you ask.

"Like nothing else," answers Scottie. "You're terrified at first, but once you're up there, you just get on with it. There's so much to think about – flying the plane, checking for bandits, keeping contact with your squadron."

"So how can you fire the guns as well?" you say.

"Good question," laughs Scottie. "The Germans fly in big formations. They come whizzing at you from all directions. You try to fix your sights on one plane, but you can't be sure of a hit. It's freezing up there, but you have to concentrate so hard, you end up soaked in sweat!"

Suddenly, you notice something. "What are those black spots?" you ask Smythe over the intercom.

"Mechanics probably forgot to clean the windows," says Smythe.

"No," you answer, firmly. "They're getting bigger!"

"Bogeys!" says Smythe. "Can you identify them?

"Looks like one's a BF109," you say. "And the other could be a Spitfire."

"You're right!" says Smythe. "Seems they're both in a spot of bother."

Black smoke is pouring from one of the planes, and the other is on fire. The next minute, two white parachutes are floating to the ground.

"I reckon they'll be needing help," says Smythe. "Let's pancake."

RAF Speak

To be a good pilot, you need to learn the language:

Planes don't take off fast, they **scramble**.

And they **pancake** when they come in to land.

You don't reach an altitude of 15,000 feet,
you fly at **angels, one five**.

Bogeys don't come from your nose. They're
unidentified aircraft.

If something's really good, it's **wizard**.

Call anyone over 25 **uncle**, or **grandad**.

Pilots aren't killed in action, for them it's
curtains.

You don't fire at the enemy, you **poop off
at the bandits**.

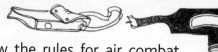

But you'd better follow the rules for air combat carefully:

- Don't fire until the enemy is in range.
- Keep looking for the enemy at all times!
- Try to keep above your enemy whenever you can.
- Always turn to face an attack.
- Think fast. Make quick decisions, even if you're wrong!
- Don't fly straight and level for more than 30 seconds.
- If you dive to attack, make sure someone covers you.
- Go in quickly – punch hard – get out!

Caterpillar Club

"Any idea where they landed?" Smythe asks as you clamber down from the Beaufighter.

"Over there, in the direction of the farm," you point, looking serious. "I'm sure I can find the place."

A group of pilots gathers around you.

"Who's missing?" asks Smythe.

"Tomasz went up about an hour ago," Buck answers.

"He's one of our finest pilots," says Smythe. "We've got to get to him fast. Who can drive?"

To your surprise, the four trained pilots all shake their heads.

"Better come with me then." Smythe climbs into a jeep. "Hop in the front," he tells you, "and I've room for two more." Scottie and Buck have to sit in the back!

You direct Smythe straight to the spot. It doesn't take you long to find Tomasz. His face is covered in mud and blood. He's clutching his nose, shaking his fist at the barn roof and shouting, "You ruined my Spitfire! Come down and finish off the fight."

You look up to see the other pilot sitting on the roof. One leg has gone right through it and the other is tied up in his parachute. He's a German! A real, live one – the first you've ever seen. But he doesn't look nasty at all. You can see he's in pain – and terrified of Tomasz.

"Why is Tomasz always so angry?" you ask Scottie.

"Well, he *has* just lost his plane and landed nose first in a cow pat," says Scottie. "But seriously, he's had things worse than the rest of us. Poland was invaded and his family starved. Tomasz risked his life to come to Britain and fight. Pilots from allied countries all over the world have done the same. Now Tomasz is only interested in one thing – revenge."

A nurse arrives and, as Scottie and Smythe help the German down, she cleans Tomasz's face and bandages his nose.

Tomasz looks more angry than ever.

"Cheer up," Buck tells him. "Do you realise you're the first in our squadron to join the Caterpillar Club?"

"What's that?" you ask.

"Anyone whose life is saved by a parachute is a member of the Caterpillar Club." Buck answers. "You get a certificate and a crawling caterpillar badge."

A police car bumps down the farm track. Two policemen jump out of the front, and rush to arrest the German pilot. A woman in a uniform steps out of the back. It's your mum!

"What are you doing here?" you ask, surprised.

"I'm on ARP duty," your mum says. "What are *you* doing here?"

You don't know where to begin. But suddenly, Smythe is shaking your mum's hand. "Squadron Leader Bentley-

Smythe," he tells her. "Is this your son?"

Your mum nods.

"Congratulations," he booms, "a fine example to all young boys. He's got courage, good sense, excellent navigational skills and eyes like a hawk. Just the sort of chap we need in the RAF. He'll be welcome in my squadron any day – er, once he's learned to fly, of course."

"That won't be for some time yet," your mum says.

Tomasz walks towards you, and he's smiling! The German pilot is lying on a stretcher ready to go to the prison hospital.

"Scottie just told me how you found us," says Tomasz. "You'll make a fine fighter pilot one day."

Everyone is saying such nice things about you, but you stop listening. You imagine yourself in years to come. You are wearing a leather jacket over your smart, blue uniform, a silk scarf round your neck, wings on your chest, and a caterpillar badge on your collar. And you are soaring through the sky in the latest Spitfire, chasing German planes back across the Channel, whilst the crowds below watch and cheer.

Being a fighter pilot is a tough job. It's scary, too, but you know you can do it.

Flying Aces – Three of the Best

There were ace fighter pilots all over the world. Some will never be forgotten:

Douglas Bader was famous because:
• He lost both his legs before the war but still became a fighter pilot
• He helped change fighter plane formation
• He shot down 22 planes, then
• He was shot down and taken prisoner
• He tried to escape so many times that the Germans threatened to take his false legs away.

Marmaduke Pattle was famous because:

- He was a brilliant shot, regularly wrecking the practice targets
- He flew with Roald Dahl, who said he was "the greatest fighter ace the Middle East was ever to see"
- He shot down about 50 enemy planes and his first 15 strikes were in an old-fashioned biplane
- He was killed in action after just nine months.

Erich Hartmann was famous because:

- His first flights were really terrible
- He crash-landed after shooting down his first plane
- But he improved quickly, shooting down 352 planes in 1400 missions
- He became the most successful fighter pilot in the world – EVER!
- He was nicknamed "the black devil" by the Russians and was captured by them when he was just 23.

Glossary

ace – a fighter pilot who has shot down five or more enemy planes

airbase – an RAF, or military, airport

airfield – where planes take off and land

air-raid – an attack on a land target by enemy planes

altitude – height at which a plane flies

ARP (Air-raid Precautions) **warden** – an official who helps others during an air raid

black out – to lose consciousness

blighter – an annoying person

bodywork – the outer structure of the plane

Bomber – a plane that carries and drops bombs

dogfight – a battle between two fighter planes

flying officer – a junior officer

formation – an arrangement of planes

gas mask – mask to protect against gas attacks

gliding – flying without using the engine

ground control – the people who monitor the aircraft from the ground

hangar – a large shed where aircraft are stored and repaired

instrument panel – the dials and controls needed to fly a plane

joystick – a stick used in controlling a plane

mess – a dining hall

mechanic – person who repairs a plane

mission – the job a pilot is sent to do

navigation – finding a place through using maps and compasses

nose – the front of the plane

oxygen – gas that is essential for human life

personnel – group of people working for the RAF

radar – device that transmits signals to show the speed and location of an object

range – distance that a gun can reach

RAF – Royal Air Force of Britain

recognition – spotting and identifying planes

recruit – person who has just joined the RAF

ripcord – a cord pulled to release a parachute

squadron – a group of planes flying under the command of one leader

taxiing – movement of a plane along the ground

Tiger Moth – a plane used to train pilots

wireless – a device that communicates information by using radio signals

WITH SO MANY **TOUGH JOBS** TO CHOOSE FROM...

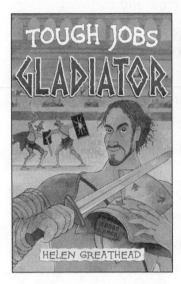

WHICH ONE WILL **YOU** TRY NEXT?